Screening and Surveillance: A Guide to OSHA Standards

U.S. Department of Labor

Occupational Safety and Health Administration

OSHA 3162-12R
2009

The Occupational Safety and Health Act requires that employers comply with safety and health standards promulgated by OSHA or by a state with an OSHA-approved state plan. This guide is a quick reference to help you locate and implement the screening and surveillance requirements of the Federal OSHA standards published in *Title 29 of the Code of Federal Regulations (29 CFR)*. This guide provides a general overview of OSHA requirements. It is not a standard or regulation, and it creates no new legal obligations. For full details of specific compliance requirements, please consult the appropriate OSHA standard in the *CFR*. You can access the medical surveillance provisions of the OSHA standards on the Internet at www.osha.gov. Additional assistance is available by telephone at 1-800-321-OSHA (6742).

Content

Glossary

BP	blood pressure
BUN	blood urea nitrogen
CBC	complete blood count
FEF	forced expiratory flow
FEV$_1$	forced expiratory volume one second
FSH	follicle stimulating hormone
FVC	forced vital capacity
HAZWOPER	Hazardous Waste Operations and Emergency Response
HBV	hepatitis B virus
LH	luteinizing hormone
MDA	methylenedianiline
PFT	pulmonary function test
PHS or **USPHS**	United States Public Health Service
PLHCP	physician or other licensed healthcare professional
PPE	personal protective equipment
SGOT	serum glutamic oxalacetic transaminase
SGPT	serum glutamic pyruvic transaminase
ZPP	zinc protoporphyrin

www.osha.gov

Acrylonitrile 1910.1045(n); 1926.1145; 1915.1045*

Standard Requirements	
Pre-placement exam	Yes[1]
Periodic exam	Yes – annual[1]
Emergency/exposure examination and tests	Yes
Termination exam	Yes – if no exam within 6 months of termination
Examination includes special emphasis on these body systems	Respiratory, gastrointestinal[1], thyroid, skin, neurological (peripheral and central)
Work and medical history	Required for all exams[2]
Chest x-ray	Yes
Pulmonary function test (PFT)	No
Other required tests	Fecal occult blood[1]
Evaluation of ability to wear a respirator	Yes
Additional tests if deemed necessary	Yes
Written medical opinion	Yes – physician to employer; employer to employee
Employee counseling re: exam results, conditions of increased risk	Yes – by physician
Medical removal plan	No

Arsenic (Inorganic) 1910.1018(n); 1926.1118; 1915.1018*

Standard Requirements

Pre-placement exam	Yes[1]
Periodic exam	Yes[1]
Emergency/exposure examination and tests	Yes
Termination exam	Yes – if no exam within 6 months of termination
Examination includes special emphasis on these body systems	Skin, nasal
Work and medical history	Required for all exams[2] with focus on respiratory symptoms; includes smoking history
Chest x-ray	Yes
Pulmonary function test (PFT)	No
Other required tests	No
Evaluation of ability to wear a respirator	Yes
Additional tests if deemed necessary	Yes
Written medical opinion	Yes – physician to employer; employer to employee
Employee counseling re: exam results, conditions of increased risk	Yes – by physician
Medical removal plan	No

# Asbestos (General Industry)
1910.1001(l)

Standard Requirements	
Pre-placement exam	Yes[1, 3]
Periodic exam	Yes – annual[1]
Emergency/exposure examination and tests	No
Termination exam	Yes – within ± 30 days of termination
Examination includes special emphasis on these body systems	Respiratory, cardiovascular, gastrointestnal
Work and medical history	Required for all exams[2] standardized form required; see standard, Appendix D
Chest x-ray	Yes[1] – B reader, board eligible/certified radiologist or physician with expertise in pneumoconioses required; see standard, Appendix E for x-ray interpretaticn and classification requirements
Pulmonary function test (PFT)	FVC, FEV_1
Other required tests	No
Evaluation of ability to wear a respirator	Yes
Additional tests if deemed necessary	Yes
Written medical opinion	Yes – physician to employer; employer to employee
Employee counseling re: exam results, conditions of increased risk	Yes – by physician; includes informing employee of increased risk of lung cancer from combined effects of smoking and asbestos exposure
Medical removal plan	No

Asbestos (Construction and Shipyards)
1926.1101(m); 1915.1001

Standard Requirements	
Pre-placement exam	Yes[1, 3]
Periodic exam	Yes – annual[1] or more frequently if determined by physician
Emergency/exposure examination and tests	No
Termination exam	No
Examination includes special emphasis on these body systems	Pulmonary and gastrointestinal
Work and medical history	Required for all exams[2]; special emphasis on pulmonary, cardiovascular, gastrointestinal; standardized form required; see standard, Appendix D
Chest x-ray	Yes[1] – B reader, board eligible/certified radiologist or physician with expertise in pneumoconioses required; see standard, Appendix E for x-ray interpretation and classification requirements
Pulmonary function test (PFT)	FVC, FEV_1
Other required tests	No
Evaluation of ability to wear a respirator	Yes
Additional tests if deemed necessary	Yes
Written medical opinion	Yes – physician to employer; employer to employee
Employee counseling re: exam results, conditions of increased risk	Yes – by physician; includes informing employee of increased risk of lung cancer from combined effects of smoking and asbestos exposure
Medical removal plan	No

Benzene
1910.1028(i); 1926.1128; 1915.1028*

Standard Requirements	
Pre-placement exam	Yes[1, 3, 4]
Periodic exam	Yes – annual[1, 4]
Emergency/exposure examination and tests	Yes[1, 4] – includes urinary phenol test
Termination exam	No
Examination includes special emphasis on these body systems	Hemopoietic; add cardiopulmonary if respiratory protection used at least 30 days/ year, (initially, then every 3 years)
Work and medical history	Required for initial and periodic exams (pre-placement exam requires special history)[2]
Chest x-ray	No
Pulmonary function test (PFT)	Initially and every 3 years if respiratory protection used 30 days/year; specific tester requirements
Other required tests	CBC, differential, other specific blood tests; repeated as required; see standard
Evaluation of ability to wear a respirator	Yes – if respirators are used
Additional tests if deemed necessary	Yes
Written medical opinion	Yes – physician to employer; employer to employee
Employee counseling re: exam results, conditions of increased risk	Yes – by physician
Medical removal plan	Yes

Bloodborne Pathogens
1910.1030(f)

Standard Requirements	
Pre-placement exam	No – must offer Hepatitis B (HBV) vaccine unless already immune or vaccine contraindicated
Periodic exam	No
Emergency/exposure examination and tests	Specific post-exposure monitoring for employee and source; HBV vaccine; see standard
Termination exam	No
Examination includes special emphasis on these body systems	No
Work and medical history	No
Chest x-ray	No
Pulmonary function test (PFT)	No
Other required tests	Yes – post-exposure incident; follow U.S. Public Health Service (USPHS) post-exposure protocols
Evaluation of ability to wear a respirator	No
Additional tests if deemed necessary	Yes – for post-exposure incident; follow USPHS post-exposure protocols
Written medical opinion	Yes – licensed healthcare professional to employer; employer to employee
Employee counseling re: exam results, conditions of increased risk	Yes – by licensed healthcare professional; counseling re: HBV vaccine and post-exposure follow-up; see standard
Medical removal plan	No

1,3-Butadiene
1910.1051(k); 1926.1151*

Standard Requirements

Pre-placement exam	Yes[1, 3, 4]
Periodic exam	Yes[1, 4]
Emergency/exposure examination and tests	Yes[1, 4] – within 48 hours of exposure
Termination exam	Yes[4] – if 12 months have elapsed since last exam
Examination includes special emphasis on these body systems	Liver, spleen, lymph nodes, and skin
Work and medical history	Required annually and for all examinations[2]; standardized form or equivalent; includes comprehensive occupational and health history; see standard, Appendices F and C
Chest x-ray	No
Pulmonary function test (PFT)	No
Other required tests	Annually, CBC with differential and platelet count; also within 48 hrs. after exposure in an emergency situation and repeated monthly for 3 more months
Evaluation of ability to wear a respirator	Yes – if respirators are used
Additional tests if deemed necessary	Yes
Written medical opinion	Yes – physician or other licensed healthcare professional to employer and employee
Employee counseling re: exam results, conditions of increased risk	Yes – by physician or other licensed healthcare professional
Medical removal plan	No

Cadmium
1910.1027(l); 1926.1127; 1915.1027; 1928.1027*

Standard Requirements	
Pre-placement exam	Yes[1, 3, 4]
Periodic exam	Yes[1, 4]
Emergency/exposure examination and tests	Yes[1, 4]
Termination exam	Yes[3] – see standard for time frame and other specifics
Examination includes special emphasis on these body systems	Respiratory, cardiovascular (BP), urinary, and for males over 40 – prostate palpation[1]
Work and medical history	Required for preplacement and periodic exams[2]; standardized form required
Chest x-ray	Yes
Pulmonary function test (PFT)	FVC, FEV_1
Other required tests	Annually[1], cadmium in urine, beta-2 microglobulin in urine, cadmium in blood, CBC, BUN, serum creatinine, urinalysis; see standard
Evaluation of ability to wear a respirator	Yes
Additional tests if deemed necessary	Yes
Written medical opinion	Yes – physician to employer; employer to employee
Employee counseling re: exam results, conditions of increased risk	Yes – by physician; includes explanation of results, treatment, and diet, and discussion of decisions re: medical removal; see standard for details
Medical removal plan	Yes

Carcinogens (Suspect)
1910.1003-1016(g); 1926.1103; 1915.1003-1016*

Standard Requirements

Pre-placement exam	Yes
Periodic exam	Yes – annual
Emergency/exposure examination and tests	Yes[1] – special medical surveillance begins within 24 hours
Termination exam	No
Examination includes special emphasis on these body systems	Exam includes determination for increased risk (e.g., treatment with steroids or cytotoxic agents. reduced immunological competence, pregnancy or cigarette smoking)
Work and medical history	Required for all examinations; includes family and occupational history, genetic and environmental factors
Chest x-ray	No
Pulmonary function test (PFT)	No
Other required tests	No
Evaluation of ability to wear a respirator	Yes – as specified in the Respiratory Protection standard, 1910.134(e), if respirators are used
Additional tests if deemed necessary	Yes
Written medical opinion	Yes – physician to employer
Employee counseling re: exam results, conditions of increased risk	No
Medical removal plan	No

Standard Requirements

Pre-placement exam	Yes[1]
Periodic exam	Yes[1]
Emergency/exposure examination and tests	Yes[1]
Termination exam	Yes[3] – unless last exam was less than 6 months prior to date of termination
Examination includes special emphasis on these body systems	Skin and respiratory tract
Work and medical history	Required for all exams[2]; includes past, present and anticipated future exposure; any history of respiratory system dysfunction, asthma, dermatitis, skin ulceration or nasal septum perforation; smoking status and history
Chest x-ray	No
Pulmonary function test (PFT)	No
Other required tests	No
Evaluation of ability to wear a respirator	Yes
Additional tests if deemed necessary	Yes
Written medical opinion	Yes – physician or other licensed healthcare professional (PLHCP) to employer; employer to employee
Employee counseling re: exam results, conditions of increased risk	Yes – by PLHCP
Medical removal plan	No

# Coke Oven Emissions
1910.1029(j)

Standard Requirements	
Pre-placement exam	Yes[1]
Periodic exam	Yes[1]
Emergency/exposure examination and tests	No
Termination exam	Yes – if no exam within 6 months of termination
Examination includes special emphasis on these body systems	Skin
Work and medical history	Required for all exams[2]; includes smoking history and presence and degree of respiratory symptoms
Chest x-ray	Yes
Pulmonary function test (PFT)	FVC, FEV_1
Other required tests	Weight, urine cytology, urinalysis for sugar, albumin, hematuria
Evaluation of ability to wear a respirator	Yes
Additional tests if deemed necessary	Yes – see standard, Appendix B
Written medical opinion	Yes – physician to employer; employer to employee
Employee counseling re: exam results, conditions of increased risk	Yes – by physician; also, employer must inform employee of possible health consequences if employee refuses any required medical exam
Medical removal plan	No

Compressed Air Environments
1926.803(b)

Standard Requirements	
Pre-placement exam	Yes
Periodic exam	Yes[1]
Emergency/exposure examination and tests	No
Termination exam	No
Examination includes special emphasis on these body systems	Not specified
Work and medical history	No
Chest x-ray	No
Pulmonary function test (PFT)	No
Other required tests	No
Evaluation of ability to wear a respirator	No
Additional tests if deemed necessary	No
Written medical opinion	No
Employee counseling re: exam results, conditions of increased risk	No
Medical removal plan	No

Standard Requirements

Pre-placement exam	Physical exam not specified; other tests required
Periodic exam	Physical exam not specified; other tests required[1, 4]
Emergency/exposure examination and tests	No
Termination exam	No
Examination includes special emphasis on these body systems	Not specified
Work and medical history	Medical history; standardized questionnaire required; see standard, Appendix B-1[1, 2, 4]
Chest x-ray	No
Pulmonary function test (PFT)	FVC, FEV$_1$, FEV$_1$/FVC Employees with specific abnormalities are referred to specialists[1, 4, 5]
Other required tests	No
Evaluation of ability to wear a respirator	Yes
Additional tests if deemed necessary	No
Written medical opinion	Yes – physician to employer; employer to employee
Employee counseling re: exam results, conditions of increased risk	Yes – by physician re: results of exam and any medical conditions requiring further examination or treatment
Medical removal plan	Yes – for inability to wear a respirator (6 months)

1,2-dibromo-3-chloropropane
1910.1044(m); 1926.1144; 1915.1044*

Standard Requirements	
Pre-placement exam	Yes
Periodic exam	Yes[1]
Emergency/exposure examination and tests	Yes – male reproductive; repeat in 3 months
Termination exam	No
Examination includes special emphasis on these body systems	Reproductive, genitourinary; see standard for details
Work and medical history	Required for all exams[2]; includes reproductive history; see standard, Appendix C
Chest x-ray	No
Pulmonary function test (PFT)	No
Other required tests	Sperm count, FSH, LH, Total estrogen (females); see standard, Appendix C for guidelines
Evaluation of ability to wear a respirator	Yes
Additional tests if deemed necessary	Yes
Written medical opinion	Yes – physician to employer; employer to employee
Employee counseling re: exam results, conditions of increased risk	Yes – by physician
Medical removal plan	No

Ethylene Oxide
1910.1047(i); 1926.1147*

Standard Requirements	
Pre-placement exam	Yes[1]
Periodic exam	Yes – annual[1]
Emergency/exposure examination and tests	Yes[1]
Termination exam	Yes[1]
Examination includes special emphasis on these body systems	Pulmonary, skin, neurologic, hematologic, reproductive, eyes
Work and medical history	Required for all exams; includes reproductive history and special emphasis on some body systems; see standard
Chest x-ray	No
Pulmonary function test (PFT)	No
Other required tests	CBC, white cell count with differential, hematocrit, hemoglobin, red cell count; if requested by employee, pregnancy testing and fertility testing (female/male) will be added to the exam as deemed appropriate by physician
Evaluation of ability to wear a respirator	Yes
Additional tests if deemed necessary	Yes
Written medical opinion	Yes – physician to employer; employer to employee
Employee counseling re: exam results, conditions of increased risk	Yes – by physician
Medical removal plan	No

Formaldehyde
1910.1048(l); 1926.1148; 1915.1048*

Standard Requirements	
Pre-placement exam	Yes[1, 4]
Periodic exam	Yes[1, 4]
Emergency/exposure examination and tests	Yes[4]
Termination exam	No
Examination includes special emphasis on these body systems	Evidence of irritation or sensitization of skin, respiratory system, eyes; shortness of breath
Work and medical history	Required for all exams[2]; questionnaire required; see standard, Appendix D
Chest x-ray	No
Pulmonary function test (PFT)	FVC, FEV_1, FEF should be evaluated if respiratory protection is used
Other required tests	No
Evaluation of ability to wear a respirator	Yes
Additional tests if deemed necessary	Yes
Written medical opinion	Yes – physician to employer; employer to employee
Employee counseling re: exam results, conditions of increased risk	Yes – by physician; includes information on whether medical conditions were caused by past exposures or emergency exposures
Medical removal plan	Yes

HAZWOPER
1910.120(f); 1926.65*

Standard Requirements	
Pre-placement exam	Yes[1]
Periodic exam	Yes – annually or at physician's discretion[1]
Emergency/exposure examination and tests	Yes[1]
Termination exam	Yes – if no exam within 6 months of termination/ reassignment
Examination includes special emphasis on these body systems	Determined by physician; see standard. Appendix D, reference 10 for guidelines
Work and medical history	Yes – with emphasis on symptoms related to handling hazardous substances and health hazards, fitness for duty and ability to wear PPE[2]
Chest x-ray	No – unless determined by physician
Pulmonary function test (PFT)	No – unless determined by physician
Other required tests	No – unless determined by physician
Evaluation of ability to wear a respirator	Yes
Additional tests if deemed necessary	Yes
Written medical opinion	Yes – physician to employer; employer to employee
Employee counseling re: exam results, conditions of increased risk	Yes – by physician
Medical removal plan	No

# Hazardous Chemicals in Laboratories
1910.1450(g)

Standard Requirements	
Pre-placement exam	When required by other standards
Periodic exam	When required by other standards
Emergency/exposure examination and tests	Yes[1]
Termination exam	No
Examination includes special emphasis on these body systems	Not specified
Work and medical history	When required by other standards
Chest x-ray	When required by other standards
Pulmonary function test (PFT)	When required by other standards
Other required tests	When required by other standards
Evaluation of ability to wear a respirator	Yes – when required by other standards
Additional tests if deemed necessary	When required by other standards
Written medical opinion	Yes – physician to employer
Employee counseling re: exam results, conditions of increased risk	Yes – by physician
Medical removal plan	No

Lead
1910.1025(j); 1926.62*

Standard Requirements	
Pre-placement exam	Yes[1, 4] except in construction industries; construction requires initial blood tests only
Periodic exam	Yes[1, 4]
Emergency/exposure examination and tests	Yes[1, 4]
Termination exam	No
Examination includes special emphasis on these body systems	Teeth, gums, hematologic, gastrointestinal, renal, cardiovascular (BP), neurological; pulmonary status if respiratory protection used
Work and medical history	Required for all exams[2]; includes reproductive history, past lead exposure, both work/non-work, and history of specific body systems; see standard
Chest x-ray	No
Pulmonary function test (PFT)	No – unless deemed necessary by physician
Other required tests	Hemoglobin, hematocrit, ZPP, BUN, serum creatinine, urinalysis with micro, blood-lead levels, peripheral smear morphology, red cell indices[1, 5]; if requested by employee, pregnancy testing and fertility testing (female/male)
Evaluation of ability to wear a respirator	Yes
Additional tests if deemed necessary	Yes
Written medical opinion	Yes – physician to employer; employer to employee

Continued on page 24

Continued from page 23

Employee counseling re: exam results, conditions of increased risk	Yes – by physician; includes advising the employee of any medical condition, occupational or non-occupational, requiring further medical examination or treatment
Medical removal plan	Yes

Methylene Chloride
1910.1052(j); 1926.1152*

Standard Requirements	
Pre-placement exam	Yes[1, 4]
Periodic exam	Yes[1, 4]
Emergency/exposure examination and tests	Yes[4] – see standard for specifics
Termination exam	Yes – if no exam within 6 months of termination
Examination includes special emphasis on these body systems	Lungs, card ovascular (including BP and pulse), liver, nervous, skin; extent of exam determined by examiner based on employee's health status, work, and medical history
Work and medical history	Required for all exams; example of work and medical history form provided in standard, Appendix B
Chest x-ray	No
Pulmonary function test (PFT)	No – unless deemed necessary by physician or other licensed healthcare professional
Other required tests	Laboratory surveillance may include tests as determined by examiner including "before and after shift tests"; see standard. Appendix B
Evaluation of ability to wear a respirator	Yes – as specified under the Respiratory Protection standard 1910.134(e)
Additional tests if deemed necessary	Yes
Written medical opinion	Yes – by physician or other licensed healthcare professional to employer and employee
Employee counseling re: exam results, conditions of increased risk	Yes – by physician or other licensed healthcare professional
Medical removal plan	Yes

Methylenedianiline
1910.1050(m)

Standard Requirements	
Pre-placement exam	Yes[1, 3, 4]
Periodic exam	Yes – annual[1, 4]
Emergency/exposure examination and tests	Yes[1, 4]
Termination exam	No
Examination includes special emphasis on these body systems	Skin, hepatic
Work and medical history	Required for all examinations[2]; includes past work with MDA and other specific items; see standard
Chest x-ray	No
Pulmonary function test (PFT)	No
Other required tests	Liver function tests, urinalysis
Evaluation of ability to wear a respirator	Yes
Additional tests if deemed necessary	Yes
Written medical opinion	Yes – physician to employer; employer to employee
Employee counseling re: exam results, conditions of increased risk	Yes – by physician
Medical removal plan	Yes

Noise
1910.95(g); 1926.52[†]

Standard Requirements	
Pre-placement exam	Baseline audiograms are required within 6 months of exposure at or above 85dB. Mobile test van exception, within one year of exposure at or above 85dB
Periodic exam	Annual audiometric testing required
Emergency/exposure examination and tests	No
Termination exam	No requirements
Examination includes special emphasis on these body systems	No
Work and medical history	No
Chest x-ray	No
Pulmonary function test (PFT)	No
Other required tests	Initial and annual audiometric testing[1, 4, 5]; see standard re: specific qualifications for the test administrator
Evaluation of ability to wear a respirator	No
Additional tests if deemed necessary	Yes
Written medical opinion	No
Employee counseling re: exam results, conditions of increased risk	Yes – if standard threshold shift or suspected ear pathology
Medical removal plan	No

Respiratory Protection
1910.134(e); 1926.103*

Standard Requirements	
Pre-placement exam	Evaluation questionnaire or exam; follow-up exam when required[5]
Periodic exam	Yes – in specific situations[5]
Emergency/exposure examination and tests	No
Termination exam	No
Examination includes special emphasis on these body systems	Yes[5] – see standard, Appendix C
Work and medical history	Yes[2] – see standard, Appendix C
Chest x-ray	As determined by physician or other licensed healthcare professional
Pulmonary function test (PFT)	As determined by physician or other licensed healthcare professional
Other required tests	As determined by physician or other licensed healthcare professional
Evaluation of ability to wear a respirator	Yes
Additional tests if deemed necessary	Yes
Written medical opinion	Yes – physician or other licensed healthcare professional to employer and employee
Employee counseling re: exam results, conditions of increased risk	Yes – by physician or other licensed healthcare professional
Medical removal plan	No

Vinyl Chloride
1910.1017(k); 1926.1117*

Standard Requirements	
Pre-placement exam	Yes[1]
Periodic exam	Yes[1]
Emergency/exposure examination and tests	Yes
Termination exam	No
Examination includes special emphasis on these body systems	Special attention to detecting enlargement of the liver, spleen or kidneys, or dysfunction of these organs and abnormalities in skin, connective tissue and pulmonary system; see standard, Appendix A
Work and medical history	Required for initial and periodic exams[2]; includes alcohol intake, history of hepatitis, exposure to hepatotoxic agents, blood transfusions, hospitalizations, and work history
Chest x-ray	No
Pulmonary function test (PFT)	No
Other required tests	Blood test for total bilirubin, alkaline phosphatase, SGOT, SGPT and gamma glutamyl transpeptidase
Evaluation of ability to wear a respirator	Yes
Additional tests if deemed necessary	Yes
Written medical opinion	Yes – physician to employer; employer to employee
Employee counseling re: exam results, conditions of increased risk	No
Medical removal plan	Yes

Footnotes

[1] Pre-placement and periodic examinations are dependent upon specific factors cited in the standard such as airborne concentrations of the substance and/or years of exposure, biological indices, age of employee, amount of time exposed per year. In addition, some standards require periodic exams to be conducted at varying time intervals. Refer to standard for complete details.

[2] Standard requires medical and work history focused on special body systems, symptoms, personal habits, and/or specific family, environmental or occupational history. Refer to standard for complete details.

[3] No examination required if previous examination done within specified time frame (e.g., 6 months or 12 months) and provisions of standard met. Refer to standard for details.

[4] Additional physician review: Some standards have provisions for referring employees with abnormalities to a specialist as deemed necessary by examiner. Other standards have provisions for multiple physician review. See specific standard for details.

[5] Standard requires specific protocol. See standard for details.

* These Maritime and Construction standards are identical to 29 CFR 1910, General Industry standards.

† 1926.52 requires an effective and continued hearing conservation program. OSHA has interpreted this to include audiograms when feasible. See Letter of Interpretation dated August 4, 1992.

OSHA Assistance

OSHA can provide extensive help through a variety of programs, including technical assistance about effective safety and health programs, state plans, workplace consultations, and training and education.

Safety and Health Management System Guidelines

Effective management of worker safety and health protection is a decisive factor in reducing the extent and severity of work-related injuries and illnesses and their related costs. In fact, an effective safety and health management system forms the basis of good worker protection, can save time and money, increase productivity and reduce employee injuries, illnesses and related workers' compensation costs.

To assist employers and workers in developing effective safety and health management systems, OSHA published recommended Safety and Health Program Management Guidelines (54 *Federal Register* (16): 3904-3916, January 26, 1989). These voluntary guidelines can be applied to all places of employment covered by OSHA.

The guidelines identify four general elements critical to the development of a successful safety and health management system:

▪ Management leadership and worker involvement,

▪ Worksite analysis,

▪ Hazard prevention and control, and

▪ Safety and health training.

The guidelines recommend specific actions, under each of these general elements, to achieve an effective safety and health management system. The *Federal Register* notice is available online at www.osha.gov.

State Programs

The *Occupational Safety and Health Act of 1970* (OSH Act) encourages states to develop and operate their own job safety and health plans. OSHA approves and monitors these plans. Twenty-five states, Puerto Rico and the Virgin Islands currently operate approved state plans: 22 cover both private and public (state and local government) em-

ployment; Connecticut, Illinois, New Jersey, New York and the Virgin Islands cover the public sector only. States and territories with their own OSHA-approved occupational safety and health plans must adopt standards identical to, or at least as effective as, the Federal OSHA standards.

Consultation Services

Consultation assistance is available on request to employers who want help in establishing and maintaining a safe and healthful workplace. Largely funded by OSHA, the service is provided at no cost to the employer. Primarily developed for smaller employers with more hazardous operations, the consultation service is delivered by state governments employing professional safety and health consultants. Comprehensive assistance includes an appraisal of all mechanical systems, work practices and occupational safety and health hazards of the workplace and all aspects of the employer's present job safety and health program. In addition, the service offers assistance to employers in developing and implementing an effective safety and health program. No penalties are proposed or citations issued for hazards identified by the consultant. OSHA provides consultation assistance to the employer with the assurance that his or her name and firm and any information about the workplace will not be routinely reported to OSHA enforcement staff. For more information concerning consultation assistance, see OSHA's website at www.osha.gov.

Strategic Partnership Program

OSHA's Strategic Partnership Program helps encourage, assist and recognize the efforts of partners to eliminate serious workplace hazards and achieve a high level of worker safety and health. Most strategic partnerships seek to have a broad impact by building cooperative relationships with groups of employers and workers. These partnerships are voluntary relationships between OSHA, employers, worker representatives, and others (e.g., trade unions, trade and professional associations, universities, and other government agencies).

For more information on this and other agency programs, contact your nearest OSHA office, or visit OSHA's website at www.osha.gov.

OSHA Training and Education

OSHA area offices offer a variety of information services, such as technical advice, publications, audiovisual aids and speakers for special engagements. OSHA's Training Institute in Arlington Heights, IL, provides basic and advanced courses in safety and health for Federal and state compliance officers, state consultants, Federal agency personnel, and private sector employers, workers and the r representatives.

The OSHA Training Institute also has established OSHA Training Institute Education Centers to address the increased demand for its courses from the private sector and from other federal agencies. These centers are colleges, universities and nonprofit organizations that have been selected after a competition for participation in the program.

OSHA also provides funds to nonprofit organizations, through grants, to conduct workplace training and education in subjects where OSHA believes there is a lack of workplace training. Grants are awarded annually.

For more information on grants, training and education, contact the OSHA Training Institute, Directorate of Training and Education, 2020 South Arlington Heights Road, Arlington Heights, IL 60005, (847) 297-4810, or see Training on OSHA's website at www.osha.gov. For further information on any OSHA program, contact your nearest OSHA regional office listed at the end of this publication.

Information Available Electronically

OSHA has a variety of materials and tools available on its website at www.osha.gov. These include electronic tools, such as Safety and Health Topics, eTools, Expert Advisors; regulations, directives and publications; videos and other information for employers and workers. OSHA's software programs and eTools walk you through challenging safety and health issues and common problems to find the best solutions for your workplace.

OSHA Publications

OSHA has an extensive publications program. For a listing of free items, visit OSHA's website at www.osha.gov or contact the OSHA Publications Office, U.S. Department of Labor, 200 Constitution Avenue, NW, N-3101, Washington, DC 20210; telephone (202) 693-1888 or fax to (202) 693-2498.

Contacting OSHA

To report an emergency, file a complaint, or seek OSHA advice, assistance, or products, call (800) 321-OSHA or contact your nearest OSHA Regional or Area office listed at the end of this publication. The teletypewriter (TTY) number is (877) 889-5627.

Written correspondence can be mailed to the nearest OSHA Regional or Area Office listed at the end of this publication or to OSHA's national office at: U.S. Department of Labor, Occupational Safety and Health Administration, 200 Constitution Avenue, N.W., Washington, DC 20210.

By visiting OSHA's website at www.osha.gov, you can also:

- File a complaint online,

- Submit general inquiries about workplace safety and health electronically, and

- Find more information about OSHA and occupational safety and health.

Region I
(CT*, ME, MA, NH, RI, VT*)
JFK Federal Building, Room E340
Boston, MA 02203
(617) 565-9860

Region II
(NJ*, NY*, PR*, VI*)
201 Varick Street, Room 670
New York, NY 10014
(212) 337-2378

Region III
(DE, DC, MD*, PA, VA*, WV)
The Curtis Center
170 S. Independence Mall West
Suite 740 West
Philadelphia, PA 19106-3309
(215) 861-4900

Region IV
(AL, FL, GA, KY*, MS, NC*, SC*, TN*)
61 Forsyth Street, SW, Room 6T50
Atlanta, GA 30303
(404) 562-2300

Region V
(IL*, IN*, MI*, MN*, OH, WI)
230 South Dearborn Street
Room 3244
Chicago, IL 60604
(312) 353-2220

Region VI
(AR, LA, NM*, OK, TX)
525 Griffin Street, Room 602
Dallas, TX 75202
(972) 850-4145

Region VII
(IA*, KS, MO, NE)
Two Pershing Square
2300 Main Street, Suite 1010
Kansas City, MO 64108-2416
(816) 283-8745

Region VIII
(CO, MT, ND, SD, UT*, WY*)
1999 Broadway, Suite 1690
PO Box 46550
Denver, CO 80202-5716
(720) 264-6550

Region IX
(AZ*, CA*, HI*, NV*, and American Samoa,
Guam and the Northern Mariana Islands)
90 7th Street, Suite 18-100
San Francisco, CA 94103
(415) 625-2547

Region X
(AK*, ID, OR*, WA*)
1111 Third Avenue, Suite 715
Seattle, WA 98101-3212
(206) 553-5930

* These states and territories operate their own OSHA-approved job safety and health programs and cover state and local government employees as well as private sector employees. The Connecticut, Illinois, New Jersey, New York and Virgin Islands plans cover public employees only. States with approved programs must have standards that are identical to, or at least as effective as, the Federal OSHA standards.

Note: To get contact information for OSHA Area Offices, OSHA-approved State Plans and OSHA Consultation Projects, please visit us online at www.osha.gov or call us at 1-800-321-OSHA.

www.ingramcontent.com/pod-product-compliance
Lightning Source LLC
Chambersburg PA
CBHW051826170526
45167CB00005B/2172